Centered

A Life Focused on Jesus

Centered

A Life Focused on Jesus

Katie Clifton

GIG Publishing

Benton, AR

Unless otherwise noted, all scripture quotations are taken from the New Living Translation.

Centered: A Life Focused on Jesus

Copyright © 2019 by Katie Clifton. All rights reserved.

Published by *GIG Publishing*, LLC.

Benton, AR.

www.GIGPublishing.com

Cover Photo taken by Katie Clifton

Author Photo taken by Katie Clifton

Cover Design by Jaketa A. McClure

Printed in the United States of America

ISBN 978-0-578-59924-3

Thank You

Thank you to the friends who have drank coffee with me (probably gallons), laughed, cried, and dug through scripture with me on this project. I learned from you. You learned from me. We learned from Jesus. You ladies are the best and this study wouldn't exist without you all desiring to know God more.

Thank you to my husband, Jared, who encouraged me when this all began. Thank you for speaking truth to me and being my fan, for talking me down when giving up on dreams feels easier and for loving me when I'm hard to love.

To my kids, I pray more than anything you love the Lord and follow Him. It is all that really matters.

To Jaketa. I am thankful that standing in the summer rain, at football camp, produced great heart conversations, but also, your willingness to take this project on to edit and publish. God Is Good and I am thankful He gave me you in my corner.

Contents

Introduction

I am so happy you have decided to commit the next 6 weeks to discovering what God has for you among His words in Hebrews.

At a time where my small group had studied several books *about* the Bible, I deeply desired to simply study a book *of* the Bible.

Whether you are simply curious as to who Jesus is and what following Him actually, means or consider yourself a seasoned disciple - the book of Hebrews beautifully connects the prophecy of the Old Testament, to the promises fulfilled through Jesus Christ, within the New Testament.

Hebrews allows us to see both history and life from God's eternal perspective.

Hebrews beautifully displays, at the center of the gospel, Jesus Christ. This study, as well as, each scripture grouping, is intended to unfold in a specific way. My prayer is that through this study, you will develop your own personal, study rhythm. Please begin each guide by first praying for the Lord to speak to you through His Word. Next, read the associated scripture passage. Jot down notes on anything that sticks out to you, questions that arise, anything that confuses you, or anything that encourages you. If you do not have a personal journal, journal pages are included in the back of your guide. These also may be used for group discussion notes.

This study was intended to do within a small group. My prayer is this group will be a safe haven. A place of friendship. A community of vulnerability and transparency. My prayer is that as you work through these first few Chapters of Hebrews, you discover the beauty of Jesus and that He will not just be a good man to you - but a Great God to you. I'd like to add that I study with NLT as my primary translation but also ESV. However, I suggest reading each verse in multiple translations. The Lord always finds a way to communicate to me through various translations.

Studying the book of Hebrews has been transformative to my relationship with the Lord and I pray it will be for you, as well.

I am so excited this little book has found its way into your hands. You are here for a reason. I believe God has something for you and I would love to hear about your experience in this study. You can find my contact information, in the back of the book, after the notes section.

Stories matter. And your story matters to me.

As much as I believe the Lord has something powerful for you, I also believe the enemy is fearful about you making the decision to commit to this study. Satan is not all knowing and his power is surely limited. But be aware - because he will certainly be on the prowl as you do this study.

The last thing Satan wants is for a woman to *center* her life on the Lord. You will become the biggest threat to his plans. You will fight with your spouse. Your kids will get sick. Your boss will move up a deadline. More will get dumped on you. Your tire will go flat. Dinner will burn. Something will happen.....*something*.

Even as I write this, my dog just threw up on the floor. Awesome.

It's not that Satan is causing all the junk to happen (we cannot give him credit he doesn't deserve), it's that he is whispering among the junk. "You can't continue with this study...You are clueless. Everyone knows more than you... You aren't worthy to be in that group... Remember when you blew up earlier... Remember that fight you had... Remember all the stress that happened today...You deserve a break... Stay home... Don't read... No one will miss you anyway... You don't belong... You weren't qualified for this."

Sound familiar? Surely, these aren't just the lies he whispers to me.

I am far too familiar with his lies.

My point is this: there will be distractions and temptations to stop along the way. I am praying you commit this time to the Lord. Center this time on Him. Commit to your group. Commit to one another. Encourage one another. And as you are faithful to see this study through, I pray the Lord does a work within you that you cannot even fathom now. I pray His Word comes alive. I pray your faith comes alive. I pray you see God move in power. I pray you become a disciple and a disciple maker. I pray you are transformed and that this study launches you into a deeper life with Jesus - A life Centered on Jesus.

This book you are holding in your hands is one that has been diligently prayed over. I believe the Lord has something for you among these pages...

and certainly not because my name is on the cover, but because the Lord has been relentless in making sure obedience happened for this book to even exist and then, to wander into your hands. Not only has this book been prayed over, but you have been prayed for on this journey, as well. I don't know the "you" whose hands are currently here, but the Lord does. He sees you. He loves you. He pursues you. He forgives you. He invites you. I pray that over these next few weeks, you not only know Him better, but you follow Him forever.

Blessings to you my friend,

Katie

Week One

Hebrews: Chapter 1

Jews who had converted to Christianity in the 1st Century, were tempted to fall back into Judaism because of their lack of understanding of Jesus being the Messiah. The familiarity of Jewish tradition/law was tempting to return to because, after all, isn't it easier to go back to what we know, rather than, live a changed life? These Jewish Christians faced heavy persecution, socially and physically, by both the Jewish people and the Romans. Even though, the Jewish people have always been God's chosen people, they reject that Jesus is the Messiah. They centered their lives on God, yet, failed to center their lives on Jesus.

Isn't it interesting that God can lavish His love so clearly on people and yet, they reject His Son? In your free time, pause and examine your heart. How have you rejected His Son? Perhaps, it is His correction you are ignoring, or maybe, it is what He is calling you to or away from?

The relationship of Christianity to Judaism was a critical issue in the early church. The author (whom we aren't clear on) is clearing up confusion by carefully explaining to the Christians how Christ is superior to the angels, Moses, and even the high priests. This truth was contrary to the years of religious training and knowledge the Jews had received. The new covenant (Jesus, His grace, mercy, and salvation) is far superior to the old covenant (keeping laws in order to receive favor from God). This new covenant was a free, gift that people could not earn.

My prayer as we study the Book of Hebrews is that we will grow in knowledge and understanding of how truly great Jesus Christ is. I pray that each one of us would be called to worship Him in new ways and with a new, refreshed, fullness of faith. I am praying God would open our minds to the truth of His Word. I am praying we abandon our attempts at striving and rest in His salvation.

Read Hebrews Chapter 1.

The following notes and questions will come from this Chapter unless another scripture is noted. Please read the corresponding passages and take notes on any truths you discover. These notes will be valuable during your group reflection.

Verse 1

Prior to the birth of Jesus, how did God speak to His people through prophets?

Read Numbers 12:6-8.

Verse 2

God promised everything to the Son as an inheritance.

Read Matthew 21:33-46.

What do you think this parable means?

Verse 3

By looking at Jesus, what can we know about the character of God?

*I found a really, great article that beautifully explains who God is. If you need a reminder about His holiness, greatness, power, and love, go to: https://bible.org/seriespage/2-what-god

Verse 3

Jesus sustains everything. Jesus is God in flesh. Do you truly view Jesus as your sustainer?

Read Colossians 1:15-22.

Verse 3

What is the significance of sitting at the right hand of God? The audience the writer was speaking to, lived in a time where Kings were very significant. What do you think this position at the right hand holds?

*Other passages referencing sitting at the right hand of God:
Psalm 110:1
Romans 8:34
Ephesians 1:19-23

Verse 4

God gave Jesus the name above all names!
Read Philippians 2:7-11.

There is power in the name of Jesus!! I found this and wanted to share it so that we can become women who truly pray with power:

*"Over and over again in Scripture we read, "In my name," "In Jesus' name," or "In his name." The demons were powerless because of his name (Luke 10:17). The demons were cast out in his name (Mark 16:17-18). Healing occurred in his name (Acts 3:6, 3:16, 4:10). Salvation comes in his name (Acts 4:12, Rom. 10:13). We are to baptize in his name (Matt. 28:19). We are justified in his name (1 Cor. 6:11). Everything we do and say is done in his name (Col. 3:17). But it is **praying in Jesus' name** that I want to bring to the forefront. Jesus has invited, urged, and commanded us to pray in his name and has promised incredible results."*

John 14:13-14 and John 16:23-24 are some of the most powerful verses in all of scripture related to prayer. In fact, when most of us pray we conclude with the phrase, "in Jesus' name." But what does it mean to pray in the name of Jesus? When we pray in Jesus' name:

1. **We are admitting the bankruptcy of our own name.**
   When I pray in Jesus' name, I come boldly before God because of the power of his name. It would be like a bride coming from abject poverty to marry a wealthy husband. At that point the woman takes the name of her husband and all that entails. She no longer acts in her name, but in his.

2. **We identify with the person of Jesus Christ.**
   Jesus has literally given us his name. When I use that name, I am confessing that He is mine and that I am His. It is like going to the bank of heaven, knowing I have nothing deposited. If I go in my name, I will get absolutely nothing. But Jesus Christ has unlimited funds in heaven's bank, and He has granted me the privilege of going to the bank with His name on my checks.

3. **We pray in His authority.**
   We are like the child who picked up a policeman's hat, wandered out onto a busy

intersection, and began to direct traffic. The people in the cars followed the child's direction because they respected his position of authority. To pray in His name, is to ask by His authority; and to ask by His authority, is to ask in accordance to his will, as revealed in His word.

4. **We submit to His will.**
   Jesus' authority rested with His submission to the Father. So, our authority rests with our submission to Him. To ask in His name, is to ask according to His nature, and His nature is one of submission. This, by the way, is why prayers that ask for things contrary to the Word of God will never be answered.

5. **We are representing Him and His interests here on earth.**
   It is much the same as the legal arrangement known as the power of attorney. In such matters, one person may represent another in his absence. They act on their behalf. Jesus has given every believer unlimited and general power of attorney in all matters, and with the right to use His name in every situation.

6. **We pray expectantly.**

When we pray in Jesus' name, we may expect the answer in accord with the value of His name. So, we can pray with great and excited expectation.

Verse 5

How does the writer of Hebrews contrast the role of the angels with the importance of Jesus?

Read Psalm 2:6-12.

Who is the Lord's chosen King? What power had the Lord given His royal Son in these verses?

Verse 5

Read 2 Samuel 7:1-14.

What promises did God make while speaking to Nathan? How is this connected to this passage in Hebrews?

Verse 6

Read Deuteronomy 32:43.

How are these passages connected to Hebrews 1:6? Do you find it amazing that God had given Moses this song in 1407 BC and the writer of Hebrews was sharing this truth in 70 AD?

Verse 7

Read Psalm 104.

Although, we aren't sure who wrote this Psalm, the Jewish audience would have been very familiar with passage. In understanding the position and importance of Jesus and the angels, we also need to focus on the power, authority, and divinity of God.

Find some time to be alone later today and read Psalm 104 again. Praise the Lord for His creativity in creation, and while He was making it all, He already knew you. He knew you would be in this Bible study and that you would meditate on His Word. Isn't it overwhelming to think that nothing surprises God?

Verses 8 & 9

Read Hebrews 1:8-9 again then, read Psalm 45. Why would the writer of Hebrews be referencing so many passages from the Old Testament? As I dug for an answer, I came across this beautiful answer:

"Hebrews has very much a 'Son' theology. And if you want to unpack who the Son is and what he does, the Psalms are a very important place to go. It is not just the songbook of Israel. It is the songbook of the Son."

Songbook of the Son. I love that. The next time you are struggling or are in a dry season of faith, turn to Psalms and meditate on the prophetic praises of Jesus Christ.

Verses 10, 11, & 12

Read Psalms 102:25-27.

The writer of Hebrews quotes these verses to show that Jesus Christ was also present and active at the creation of the world. When you think of, "In the beginning" (Genesis 1:1), do you think of the Trinity (Father, Son, Spirit) as the Creator of the heavens and the earth? Read Genesis 1:26. Who is the "us" God is speaking to? Who is the "our" He is referring to? It can be easy for me to only see God is the Father, Jesus is the Son and Savior, and the Holy Spirit is my helper. Yes, they are 3 BUT, they are 3 IN 1. Wherever God is, all 3 parts of Him are. He cannot be divided. I get wrong theology in my head when I begin to see them as separate or unequal.

Verse 13

In Psalm 110:1, David calls the awaited Messiah his "Lord". In Matthew 22:41-46, religious leaders began questioning Jesus, and Jesus refers to David's psalm. The Pharisees (Jews) knew that the Messiah would be a descendant of David and, therefore, held David with high regard. Jesus quotes Psalm 110:1 to show these religious leaders that the Messiah would be even greater than David. The most important question we will ever answer is what we believe about Christ. Who do you say Jesus is? How does your life reflect your belief? Is He your *Center*?

Whatever you are considering as the focus of your life (marriage, work, kids, hobbies, wealth, status, etc...) **Christ is better**. He is higher than the angels. He is the perfect revelation of God, the complete and final sacrifice for sin, the compassionate and understanding mediator, and the **only** way to eternal life. May we be women who believe this. May we be women who display this.

Week Two

Hebrews: Chapter 2:1-4

In our first week of digging through Hebrews, scripture has taught us that Christ is better. He is higher than the angels. He is the perfect revelation of God, the complete and final sacrifice for sin, the compassionate and understanding mediator, and the **only** way to eternal life. Christ is who our lives should be centered on.

Today, we will begin our study of Chapter 2. In this chapter the writer of Hebrews teaches us lessons from Christ's humanity. Jesus is the perfect human leader and He wants to lead you. Jesus is the holy model set before us and He is who our lives should conform to. Jesus is our perfect sacrifice and He died for you and for me. By defeating the grave, Jesus taught us that He is our conqueror. Jesus is our High Priest and final atonement, giving us full and unending access to the throne of God.

Read Hebrews 2:1-4.

The following notes/questions will come from these 4 verses unless another passage of scripture is noted. Please take the time to write down any thoughts or experiences you have from these passages.

Verse 1

Many translations of this passage begin with "Therefore," (some translations say "so now"). I have always heard that in scripture, when we see the word therefore, we need to ask, "What is it there for?" Here, the introduction is referring to the truth of Hebrews Chapter 1. It's like saying, "Because of all of that, pay attention to all of this. *Listen* to what you have *heard* or..."

Hearing is simply the act of perceiving sound by the ear. If you are not *hearing*-impaired, *hearing* simply happens. It is involuntary. *Listening*, however, is something you consciously choose to do. *Listening* requires concentration so that your brain processes meaning from words and sentences. If someone is instructing us, then we process those words and sentences and once we apply the direction, we move into action.

"Listen": Read James 1:22-25.

Listening without obeying was like what, according to James? How does James say God honors obedience?

The word "or," in verse 1, is used to link alternatives. Listen *OR* drift away. "Or" means there will be a consequence for actions or a choice to make. If we do not listen to the truth that we have heard, *then* we will drift away. Consequential statements also come in If/Then formats.

One of my favorite If/then sections of scripture is found in John 15:1-17 (read). What are the benefits of abiding (remaining) in Jesus? What are the consequences of not abiding in Jesus?

"Drift away": Read Revelation 2:4-5.

One writer said, "That church's experience 2,000 years ago intersects our lives in this way: *drifting is the besetting sin of our day.* And as the metaphor suggests, it is not so much intentional as from unconcern. Christians neglect their anchor – Christ – and begin to quietly drift away. There is no friction, no dramatic sense of departure. But when the winds of trouble come, the things of Christ are left far behind, even out of sight."

The writer of Revelation uses a different language but refers to the same thing when he says to the ostensibly healthy Ephesian church, "Yet I hold this against you: You have forsaken your first love."

What keeps a boat at sea from drifting away? Read Hebrews 6:18-20.

How does this apply to Hebrews 2:1?

Verse 2

Read Acts 7:51-60.

Acts is an accurate historical record of the early church. After Jesus' death, burial, and resurrection, His disciples set out to expand the gospel like Christ commanded. Acts is also a theological book, with lessons and living examples of the work of the Holy Spirit, the do's and don'ts of church relationships/organization, the implications of grace, and the law of love. Acts is also an Apologetic work, which builds a strong case for the validity of Christ's claims as the Son of God and His promises to us.

In these verses from Acts, we again see that angels are messengers from God and that as the angels delivered the law (which these Jewish leaders were fully aware of), punishment was carried out for disobedience. Rules and consequences, more if/then situations. These were things the Jewish leaders were extremely familiar with. *And yet they were deaf to the truth*...again, they heard truth, but they did not listen. Stephen called out the Jewish leaders for their sin (vs 51-53) when he reminded them, they were ignoring the message God has sent to them through His angels. The Jews were infuriated.

Their reaction may seem severe to us. But....

How do we feel when we are called out in our sin? Mad, right? Embarrassed? Uncomfortable? Defensive? Where do you think these emotions come from? Pride? Self-righteousness? Shame?

In contrast to drifting away, we get to see perseverance in these verses from Acts. Perseverance is holding fast (that beautiful anchor of hope), and Stephen was steadfast. His faith was unwavering. He was known for the Holy Spirit's presence in His life. (Wouldn't that be a beautiful legacy for you to leave?) He was faithful unto death and died for sake of claiming truth. In fact, Stephen was the first Christian martyr.

How quickly do we sell out for less? How quick are we to find ways to justify or compromise to sin, rather than stand firm on the Word of God? And what was the fruit of Stephen's faithfulness in these verses?

Believers became heavily persecuted and they scattered to different regions. With their move, they expanded the reach of the gospel: persecution, divide, multiply. This is the great commission (Matthew 28:16-20)

Ultimately, because of the death of Stephen, Saul enters the picture and "uttered threats with every breath and was eager to kill the Lord's followers" (Acts 9:1). As Saul set out to arrest more followers of Jesus, the Lord met him on the road to Damascus. We know that Saul becomes Paul, one of the greatest missionaries in history and is also the greatest contributing author of the New Testament.

If God can take Saul, a non-believing, murdering, persecutor of Christianity, and *choose* him for Kingdom work, then, God is able to transform the soul of any person. No one is beyond the reach of the transforming power of Jesus. Not even you, sister.

This a beautiful reminder that we do not have to be good enough to earn the grace of God. God gives us underserved favor. Thank You, Jesus!

Verse 2 says (translated by Katie ☺):

We know what messages God delivered through the angels, and every time the law was given to them, and was disobeyed, punishment was given. If you paid attention to what I already spoke to you, and believe that Jesus is far superior to the angels, then (verse 3), why would you not take even more seriously the Word given to you by Jesus - who has been proven to be far greater than all the angels?!" Consider this as we dig into verse 3 of Hebrews 2.

Verse 3

Since *every* violation of the law brings punishment (verse 2), why would you (*insert your name here*) think you can escape punishment?

Eyewitnesses to Jesus' ministry have handed down His teachings which are in the Bible you hold in your hands. Just like the second-generation believers in Hebrews (which is who this original audience was made of), we have not seen Jesus personally.

When we do not ignore this great salvation, Jesus says, "Blessed are those who believe without seeing Me" (John 20:29).

Many people question scripture and look for ways to find error among the pages, but *IF* we believe that God is holy, full of infinite knowledge, eternal, faithful, and sovereign, then, we can trust His Word *IS* His infallible Word.

The New Testament Scriptures are the teaching of Jesus. It is God's revelation *to men* that was **"first communicated through the Lord."** This is entirely consistent with our Lord's teaching. God tells us in the Book of John, He will communicate to us, what He desires us to know.

God sent Jesus as our salvation and then conveyed His message to us by those who heard Him directly. For this reason, the New Testament writers speak with authority.

Read John 1:14-18 & 1John 1:1-4.

How do John's words confirm that Jesus announced salvation and then, used disciples to deliver the message of the truth?

Read 2Peter 1:16-21.

What does Peter say that would lead us to believe he is a reliable witness? How are these passages connected to Hebrews 2:3?

The truth of verse 3: A greater Word, brought to us by a greater Person (Jesus), having greater promises than any profit or angel before Him, will bring a greater condemnation if neglected. The Lord has revealed Himself to us and confirmed the truth of His teaching by giving His message to the disciples.

Verse 4

The Lord has had me so excited to study this verse with you. Sometimes when I study, the Word truly comes alive to me and the Lord speaks new things into my Spirit. This happened for me with this passage. I am praying now that the Lord reveals something specific to each one of us today.

God confirms Jesus' words by providing signs and miracles. In the book of Acts, miracles and gifts of the Spirit authenticated (proved by evidence) the Good News wherever it was preached. Gifts of the Spirit display the presence of God.

Read Acts 9:31-43.

What "signs and wonders, miracles and gifts" are displayed in this passage?

In verse 34 of Acts 9, Peter says, "Jesus Christ heals you!" We learned in Hebrews 1 that God gave Jesus the name above all names and that Jesus is better than everything. This miracle not only authenticates the gospel of Jesus, but it displays the healing power of His Name **by those who are led by the Spirit.**

Did you catch that? *Nonbelievers do not use the name of Jesus with any authority.* It is only His people, led by His Spirit, that can accomplish the work He has called them to.

In verse 36 of Acts 9, Tabitha is introduced. Doesn't Tabitha sound like an incredible woman? She was always doing kind things for others and helping the poor. She had opened her heart to Jesus, and this changed everything for her. In fact, Tabitha is the only woman in the Bible who is named to be a disciple of Jesus. It was out of gratitude for Jesus that she dedicated her gift to be used for God's Kingdom. Her gifts of kindness, compassion, and service were all gifts of the Spirit. Since the Lord had given her the gift and ability to sew, she used her gift for His glory. True love expresses itself in deeds and not words (1John 3:18).

Read James 1:27 and compare it with the passage from Acts 9. What pure and faultless ways did Tabitha display her faith?

Some people like Peter and Paul have been given the gift of preaching or healing. Our gifts are all different, but each person who is made new by the Holy Spirit possesses gifts from the Spirit.

Read 1Corinthians 12:1-31.

God is completely involved in the giving, using and empowering of gifts. We are responsible to use and sharpen our gifts, but we cannot take credit for what God has freely given us. As you seek to identify and utilize the gifts God has given you, make loving God and His people your highest motive. What has the Lord given you the ability to do? What do you enjoy doing? What are you passionate about? How can you use your gift for Jesus?

If you have accepted salvation through the blood of Jesus Christ and are not sure of what your gifts are, pray and ask the Lord to show you how He wants to use you and then, as the Spirit leads, be obedient. He will reveal your gifts. There is also a great online evaluation which can help us better identify how God has gifted us. You can find it here: https://spiritualgiftstest.com.

In verses 38 & 39, when Tabitha became sick and died, her body was prepared for burial. During this time, the believers (widows), whom she had influenced, went to track down Peter. They asked him to, "Come as soon as possible!" Verse 39 says. "And Peter returned with them." He entered the room filled with the widows Tabitha had shown compassion to. They were weeping and proudly clinging to the gifts she had given them.

Y'all! Let's not miss this. I don't know about you, but a lot of people need me *and* they need me *a lot*. So when someone (confession, it's usually my kids, but it has also been my husband, friends, and...God) comes running up and says, "Come with me, we need you," I do not always go. Because I *think* I am too busy. I am busy doing 100 things, most of which, I feel like should have been done yesterday. I know I am not alone in this.

As we examine these 2 verses, I don't want us to miss a quality that Peter had. It is a quality that the Lord values greatly: **AVAILABILITY**.
If we are "too busy" and do not make ourselves available to God, it will not matter what kind of ability He has given us. Without availability, our gifts are of no value. So, what does it mean to you, to be available for God?

For me, it means we pour ourselves out as a sacrifice for Him. We give Him our ears to hear, and we ***listen and obey*** His commands. We give Him our time so that we can serve Him. We give ourselves completely, fully and wholly for God, to do ***anything*** and ***everything*** He wants to do in us, through us, with us, and even, for us. It means, He is our center.

Had Peter said, "Hang on a minute. I will be there soon. Just let me finish this first..." maybe, it would have been too late. Maybe, Peter would have totally missed an opportunity to RAISE SOMEONE FROM THE DEAD. What a thing to be used for! Because, Peter made himself available, Tabitha was brought back to life, the widows were given back their friend, and "The news spread through the whole town, and many believed in the Lord," (verse 42). The next time we find ourselves "too busy", let's hit the pause button and ask God to make us available for His glory. As Christ followers, it is for His glory that we live.

In Acts 9:40, Peter asks to be alone and then, he kneels to pray. I want us to look closely at the power of Peter's posture and Peter's prayer. I found this beautiful article and wanted to share it.

Peter's Posture:

"One thought about the origin of kneeling to pray comes from the practice of kneeling before a king in petition for a request. This tradition was a symbol of humbleness and honor when coming before a king or ruler. In recognition and honor to God, it may have been the appropriate position to come before Him."

The Bible shows us many positions for prayer. We read in the Bible that Jesus did kneel when He prayed. Jesus was accompanied by His disciples as they prayed on the Mount of Olives. There were also times He prayed in a standing position as the disciples asked Him to teach them how to pray. Jesus instructed them in what we call the Lord's Prayer (Matthew 6:9-13). "There," He told them, "Pray that you will not be overcome by temptation." He walked away, about a stone's throw, and knelt down and prayed" (Luke 22:40-41).

Sometimes, prayer is spontaneous and takes a variety of physical positions. All of these examples illustrate acceptable ways of prayer. Scripture commands us to **proclaim God's greatness by means of our bodies.** (Whoa! This could be a whole other topic of study. How beautiful is that)! Here are a few additional examples of ways God is pleased with our worship.

- Some danced and sang their prayers as Miriam did (Exodus 15:20).
- The Israelites bowed their heads in gratitude and worship (Exodus 12:27).
- Job fell to the ground to petition God (Job 1:20).
- The Levites stood and praised the Lord with a loud shout (2 Chronicles 20:19).
- "For the choir director: A psalm of the descendants of Korah. Come, everyone, and clap your hands for joy! Shout to God with joyful praise!" (Psalm 47:1).
- "Come, let us worship and bow down. Let us kneel before the LORD our maker" (Psalm 95:6).
- "Praise his name with dancing, accompanied by tambourine and harp" (Psalm 149:3). "So wherever you assemble, I want men to pray with holy hands lifted up to God, free from anger and controversy" (1 Timothy 2:8).

We see clapping, shouting, kneeling, dancing, playing instruments, standing in awe, raising hands, and lying down. Clearly, all these actions are acceptable and appropriate in the worship of God. God is pleased and hears our prayers no matter how we pray. The important thing is that we come to Him in **humbleness** and with a **sincere** and **submissive** heart. I believe the Lord welcomes and honors a physical posture of humility and bankruptcy (from Hebrews Chapter 1 notes).

Peter's Prayer

After Peter cleared the room, he prayed and then, called out, "Tabitha arise!"

What I want us to think about is how Peter must have felt in this situation.

Would we have known what to say? Did he know he would have the gift to bring Tabitha back to life? How did Peter know what to do or what to say? I believe he made himself so available to the Lord that he was purely operating out of faith and obedience. He allowed himself to be an instrument of the Holy Spirit.

Peter did not have the healing power, but he was filled with the Spirit of God, who has unlimited power. Peter wasn't the one to resurrect Tabitha, God was. Peter had been 1 of the chosen 12 disciples who followed Jesus, traveled with Him, and experienced the power and authority God had given Jesus. Peter was with Jesus after the resurrection and witnessed His ascension into Heaven. Since Peter was a student, follower, and friend of Jesus (I am assuming), he would have witnessed the miracle in Mark 5:30-43. **Read this passage.

As I studied, read and compared these passages, I couldn't help but notice the words of Jesus in Mark 5 as He called *"Talitha koum"* which means "child arise," and if Peter was speaking Aramaic (after researching this, many people smarter than me believe Peter would have) he would have called *"Tabitha koum"*. That is almost the same phrase!!

A good disciple follows their master and that is exactly what Peter did here. In Luke 6:40, Jesus said, "Disciples are not greater than their teacher. But the disciple who is fully trained will become like the teacher." Peter copied what he had seen the

Lord do in a similar situation. Being obedient to Jesus will allow us to reflect the glory of the Lord.

Read 2Corinthians 3:18.

How beautiful and encouraging are these words?

This week, I am praying that we have clearly seen God's greatness displayed through His Word. I am praying we are challenged to make ourselves available to be used by God and for God. I am praying we grow deep roots downward (anchor), so that we can bear fruit upward. I pray the Lord would unveil our eyes so that we can see "the signs and wonders and various miracles and gifts of the Holy Spirit," both in His Word and in our daily lives.

I pray we continue to grow in the knowledge, power, and understanding of the greatness of Jesus, as we center our lives on Him. I pray the Lord continues to open our minds to the beautiful relationship of the Trinity, and that we might dethrone anything we have placed higher than God, including the use of our time. Lord, give us the ability to understand your Word in fresh, new ways each day. Give us understanding and wisdom. Make us learn to listen to your Spirit and give us the strength and perseverance to obey You.

In Jesus' Name.
Amen.

Week Three

Hebrews: Chapter 2:5-10

So far, in Hebrews, the writer has clarified that Jesus is higher than any prophet, higher than all the angels, and higher than any created being. Jesus is both the Son of God *and* is equal to God. He is the radiance of the glory of God and the exact representation of God's nature. God has anointed Jesus by pouring out the oil of joy on Him, more than anyone else (Hebrews 1:9). Jesus was there at creation (He is the beginning) Jesus is God's final and decisive Word to the world (He is the end). He is eternal and will remain forever (Hebrews 1:10).

The writer reminded the original audience of what they knew: The Old Covenant, which had been delivered through angels and prophets, and whenever the law was disobeyed, punishment was given. If they knew to obey the "law," and understood the consequences of disobedience, then, how much more should they understand the New Covenant of grace and the consequence of rejecting Jesus as the only source of Salvation.

This week we will focus on the glorious humanity of Jesus Christ based on scripture and the connection we can experience with Him because of His humanity.

Read Hebrews 2:5-10.

The following notes/questions will come from these 4 verses unless another passage of scripture is noted. Continue to take notes on any observations and experiences you have as you study.

Verse 5

Angels, being lower than Jesus, will have no authority, power, jurisdiction or control over the future world, "of which we are speaking" or "that we are talking about". This introduction literally means, I am telling you about the world to come and you need to pay attention because these angels you hold with such high esteem will be powerless. Jesus rules over all creation, now and in the future.

Verse 6-8

Read Psalm 8, Job 7:16-17, & Genesis 1:26-28.

Why is man so important to God? Why do you think God would delegate earthly authority to man? What does He expect man to do with the authority He entrusted them/us with?

If scripture says God has made man in His image, what does this mean about Jesus?
In Hebrews 1, we discussed "wrong theology," regarding the Trinity.

It is scripturally wrong to think of Jesus as merely God or merely man. It is wrong to think of Him as 50% God, 50% man (or any other percentage split). It is wrong to think of Him as "man on the outside" and "God on the inside." The Bible teaches, Jesus is *fully* God and *fully* man. One writer said, "His human nature was added to His divine nature, and both natures existed in one Person, Jesus Christ."

We have also discussed the importance of who we say Jesus is. There have always been false teachings about Jesus. One of the theories of Jesus at this time in history was, He wasn't God, but that He also wasn't really, human and He only *seemed* to be human. This heresy is called *Docetism*: The belief that Jesus Christ did not actually die, and therefore was never resurrected.

Read 1John 4:2 & 1John 5:6-12.

I wanted to share with you a fantastic site to recap everything we have discussed so far, as well as, give you more insight to the historical thought that Jesus was just an angel: http://www.desiringgod.org/messages/jesus-christ-infinitely-superior-to-angels

Verse 8, that God has given man authority over ALL THINGS. What does this mean about Jesus?

Read Matthew 19:28-30 & Matthew 24: 30-31.

Why do you think Jesus calls himself the Son of Man? Why is the manhood of Jesus Christ so valuable to us?

Read John 19:11.

Where does Jesus say all authority and power comes from? How would Jesus rule and reign over the world to come, if He is not human, since God has given man authority over all things on earth? God's promise to put the world under subjection to man is true, because Jesus is a man.

Verse 8 presents the problem with what we have **not** seen: "But we have not yet seen all things put under their (man's) authority." What do you think some of the not yet seen things, may be?

Verse 9 presents the solution with what we **can** see: "But we see Jesus," and He was given a position, "a little lower than the angels".

Ok. Wait. Pause.

We have been reading over and over about how Jesus is greater than angels, higher than angels and far superior to all the angels. What do you think "lower than the angels" mean?

In Christ's willingness and humility, He was given to us as a human, man. He emptied Himself and took on a posture of sacrifice and endured suffering, for us.

Read Philippians 2:6-11.

Verse 10

Read Romans 5:12-21.

Because Jesus was able to suffer, what must this mean about Him? (Consider some of the ideas about Jesus at the time Hebrews was written). How was Jesus made a perfect leader through suffering? According to the passage in Romans, what gift did Jesus' suffering offer humanity?

It was only through the sacrifice of the perfect Lamb of God (Jesus), that grace could enter into the world. **Suffering brought us grace**. Christ was willing to suffer in obedience to the Father's will, and it was through suffering, that Jesus completed the work necessary for our own salvation. **Suffering brought us salvation.**

Jesus was "perfected" by sufferings, which means, when He took on flesh, He "became uniquely qualified" to be our substitute, as one of us. It does not mean that there ever was fault with God the Son. The issue is, in order to save humanity—God's image-bearers—He had to become a man to be able to save man. This is the greatest example of grace upon grace.

Since grace is a byproduct of suffering, consider the ways you have experienced suffering in your own life. How have you suffered the greatest? Do you notice in the same areas where you have experienced suffering, those are also the areas where you experience the most empathy and compassion? Take some time to reflect on this and please share and discuss this during your small group time this week.

2Timothy 3:12 says that everyone who wants to live a godly life for Christ, will suffer.

Read Romans 8:23.

We long for our bodies to be released from earthly suffering, as we wait - *with eager hope* - for the redemption of our bodies, as we are brought into salvation by Jesus. As Christians experience and endure suffering, suffering refines our faith. The Bible addresses the many ways suffering can come upon us.

Read 2Corinthians 4:8-10.

What types of suffering does Paul mention in these verses? If you are a believer, then, *when* suffering occurs, it should happen in community. You should not suffer alone. The body of Christ was designed to suffer together. The church should always be a refuge for the hurting.

Read Galatians 6:2.

Suffering of various kinds equips us for ministry.

Read 2Corinthians 1:3-7.

From this passage, why does the Lord comfort us in all of our troubles?

I found this wonderful excerpt from a Christian author on suffering:

"When you've passed through your own fiery trials and found God to be true to what he says, you have real help to offer. You have firsthand experience of both his sustaining grace and his purposeful design. He has kept you through pain; he has reshaped you more into his image. What you are

*experiencing from God, you can give away in
increasing measure to others. You are learning both
the tenderness and the clarity necessary to help
sanctify another person's deepest distress."*

There is something about this that makes
suffering seem bitter-sweet and beautiful to me. I
wonder how many opportunities I have missed, in
the midst of, suffering, because my focus was on *my*
problems and *my* pain, rather than how God might
use it for His glory and for my comfort. With Christ as
our center, our sufferings have purpose.

I am thankful that when God suffered, He
thought of me *and* He thought of you. It was His love
and submission that held Him to the cross, not nails
and certainly, not man.

In, "Walking With God Through Pain and
Suffering," Timothy Keller writes, "While other
worldviews lead us to sit in the midst of life's joys,
foreseeing the coming sorrows, Christianity
empowers its people to sit in the midst of this
world's sorrows, tasting the coming joy."
What sorrows are you sitting in now? What joy can
you look forward to in this moment?

Suffering is also a spiritual battlefield.
Wherever suffering is, there is a battle waging for
your soul. When we suffer, we have 2 choices to
make:

Will I turn **to** God in this storm? OR will I **turn
away** from God?

I have seen many dear friends face
heartaches, pain, and loss through their suffering.
Many of them emerged refined like gold in a fire, but
others have allowed their faith to turn to ashes. They

drifted away (Hebrews 2:1), in the midst of suffering. Suffering prepares us for more glory.

Read 2Corinthians 4:13-18.

Our present troubles produce for us a glory that will last forever. Paul says, in Verse 18, that the troubles we now see, are transient or temporary, but the unseen things are eternal.

Before we end, I want us to compare this passage in 2Corinthians, with a verse we studied earlier in this week's lesson: Hebrews 2:8-9. What connection is there between what we do see and do not see in these passages?

God has appointed Jesus and crowned Him with glory and through the suffering and death of Jesus we can have the hope of eternal salvation. We do not yet see Jesus reigning on earth, but we can picture Him in His heavenly glory. When we find ourselves overwhelmed by circumstances, broken through suffering or anxious about the future, we need to reflect on the authority and position of Jesus (Hebrews 2:8-9). Where is His authority and position in your life?

Friends, Jesus is Lord of all, and He will rule this earth just as He does now in heaven.

I pray that through our suffering, He will make us holy as He is holy. I pray that we pour ourselves out daily, with thankfulness for the suffering of Jesus that brought us salvation. I pray that the Lord would continue to open our eyes and ears and increase our understanding so that we will listen and not drift away from this truth we have heard. I pray the Lord will expose our spiritual gifts to each of us and that we would obediently use them for the glory of God. I pray that He anoints each of us with His oil of joy and that a lost and dying world would see the fruit of our faith, as we remain in Him, our lives centered on Him, both now and forever. Amen.

Week Four

Hebrews: Chapter 3

This week we will dig our way through Chapter 3 of Hebrews. The writer has been clearly focused on authenticating the holiness, humanity, and righteousness of Jesus. We are reminded to listen carefully to the truth that we have heard, or we will drift away from Jesus. Consider all the things/voices you listen to daily. Which is louder? Culture or truth? Criticism or truth?

The original audience of Hebrews were criticized heavily by the Jewish culture around them and the pagans must have thought they were crazy. The Hebrews were enduring great social/spiritual suffering and persecution. It was important that the writer express to the readers that Jesus is greater than Moses. Everything in the entire Jewish system and Jewish religion had been given through Moses, to them. The Hebrew audience needed understanding of Messianic truths. The writer knew that the Hebrews needed encouragement to press on in their faith. They needed endurance.

Read Hebrews 3.

The following notes/questions will come from this chapter, unless, another passage of scripture is noted.

Verse 1

Read Leviticus 20:26.

Belonging to God means we have been set apart, made holy, as He is holy.

Read Ezekiel 16:1-22.

Examine this passage. What did the Lord provide for Jerusalem when she became the Lord's (Verses 9-14)?

Because of Jerusalem's sin and unfaithfulness, the Lord's holy presence could not remain in their temple. What use is a *temple* without the Lord?

Read 1Corinthians 6:19-20.

How does this passage relate to us belonging to the Lord?

Verse 1

Some translations of this passage use the word "consider," while others use "think carefully." What does consider mean to you?

As holy people, we are told to consider Jesus. The verb consider primarily means a mental action: to examine, ponder, or meditate on. The Greek word includes the idea of sight. Consideration, in this context, means to fix one's eyes on, to continue to focus on, or give attention to. The verb is in present tense, so it symbolizes continuing action.

Isn't that beautiful? Examine with your head, grow and keep growing in knowledge, then keep your eyes -today, tomorrow and forever- centered on Jesus.

Meditations on "Consider Jesus," by Octavius Winslow, is a 31, topic devotional on the things we should consider about Jesus. In your personal study time, I encourage you to take time to consider all that Jesus is.

http://www.preceptaustin.org/hebrews_31-4

Verse 1-6

Matthew Henry, a pastor and preeminent Bible commentator, wrote this, in regards to this passage of scripture:

*"Christ is to be considered as the Apostle of
our profession, the Messenger sent by God to men,
the great Revealer of that faith which we profess to
hold, and of that hope which we profess to have.*

*As Christ, the Messiah, anointed for the office
both of Apostle and High Priest.*

*As Jesus, our Saviour, our Healer, the great
Physician of souls. Consider him thus. Consider what
he is in himself, what he is to us, and what he will be
to us hereafter and forever. Close and serious
thoughts of Christ bring us to know more of him. The
Jews had a high opinion of the faithfulness of Moses,
yet his faithfulness was but a type of Christ's. Christ
was the Master of this house, of his church, his
people, as well as their Maker. Moses was a faithful
servant; Christ, as the eternal Son of God, is rightful
Owner and Sovereign Ruler of the Church.*

*There must not only be setting out well in the
ways of Christ, but steadfastness and perseverance
therein to the end. Every meditation on his person
and his salvation, will suggest more wisdom, new
motives to love, confidence, and obedience."*

The rich knowledge of Jewish history these
Christians held would likely have tempted them to
exalt Moses to a place of honor, that only Jesus
should hold.

Read Exodus 14:15-31.

In what miraculous ways was Moses used by
the Lord in this passage? Specifically, what miracles
do we see God performing through Moses here?

Write down some of the miracles of Jesus
from the gospels Matthew, Mark, Luke and John.

Moses was used _by God_. Jesus _is God_.

Verse 6

The word "house" is used 6-7 times (varying by translations) in this passage. House is a metaphor for God's people, in which, the Holy Spirit takes residence. There is a difference in being the House of God and being in the house of God.

"The Most High doesn't live in temples made by human hands..." Acts 7:48.

What does being the "House of God" mean in your life?

Verse 7-11

We are warned to not harden our hearts, rebel, or test the Lord.

Read Exodus 17:1-7.

Repeatedly, we see the Israelites complaining about their problems, rather than praying and relying on the faithfulness of God. How often do you live as if you are questioning, "Is the Lord here with us or not?"

Discuss what you may be experiencing in this current season. Are you facing a challenge? Are you lonely? Is your marriage struggling? Is addiction overtaking a loved one? Do you have big decisions to make?

We are to share our struggles and bear one another's burdens. We all have moments where we wonder where the Lord is. Now is the time to share, confess, and to love one another as members of one body.

Verse 12-13

The writer changes the tone of this letter with this exhortation. Exhortation means to emphatically urge someone to do something. The author says, "Be careful then", encourage one another, fighting the deception of sin (evil, unbelieving, and turning away), which leads to a hardened heart.

The word unbelieving in verse 12 is, in contrast to, the example of the faithfulness, presented by Moses and Jesus, in Hebrews 3:1–6. When we are "unbelieving," our unbelief is demonstrated in a lack of obedience to God.

Do you consider your personal lack of obedience to God as unbelief?

Meditate on this question. Journal your thoughts. Prepare to share and discuss in what areas the Lord has exposed your unbelief.

The lack of belief/obedience would result in drifting away (Hebrews 2:1), a term used to describe someone moving from an anchor point (the living God). One Bible scholar interpreted this drifting, "not as becoming a classic apostate or one who leaves Christianity, rather in this context it seems best to interpret "drifting" as rebelling against God."

The Christians of this time probably thought they were becoming more spiritual by adding in certain beliefs about angels or thinking that trusting in Moses, as well as, Jesus was a move towards Christian growth. I imagine this faith drift seemed innocuous, but it leads to a path of hybrid faith. The author of Hebrews cared greatly about the faith development of the audience and did not want them, or us, to be led astray or devoted to a diluted faith.

Verse 12

The audience was "brothers and sisters." This book was written for *all* believers as a source of truth and encouragement.

Verse 13

This verse addresses Christian community and the importance of communion with the body of Christ. *Accountability* is the anecdote to developing a heart of unbelief that results in disobedience and rebellion to God.

Who are you "warning" in life?

Who is "warning" you?

Verse 14

What do you think it means for you to live a life faithful to the end? Share and discuss.

What could a faithful life, centered on Jesus, accomplish for the Kingdom?

Dream BIG here. How could God use you? What crazy, God-sized dreams have been planted in you? What could happen if you allowed those dreams to be cultivated?

Verse 15-19

The particular "rest" referred to here was that of the land of Canaan. God said the Israelites who disobeyed Him would never enter His rest (Hebrews 3:11). They had been rebellious. All of His attempts at caring for them, protecting them, going before them, leading them, providing for them, and reclaiming them had failed.

God caused His mercy to pass over them and gave them just judgments for all their rebellion. The ultimate judgement was that they would never enter the Promised Land (Hebrews 3:16–19).

Read Numbers 14:1-25.

Read Psalm 95 and compare the chapter with Hebrews 3:15-19.

A hardened heart is as useless as dried out clay. It crumbles under pressure. It takes no shape in the creator's hand. The writer is warning us not to harden our hearts and take the Lord for granted as the Israelites did. When we disregard the will of God in our life and lose faith in Him, He will spit us from His mouth.

How can a Christian wrestle with God, even be angry with God, yet cling to their faith? What do you think this looks like lived out?

Verse 19

"Unbelief kept them from entering God's rest." Again, examine Psalm 95. This chapter contains the recipe for entering into God's blessing. His rest.

- Praise the Lord for salvation through Jesus (Psalm 95:1).
- Be full of thankfulness and praise (Psalm 95:2).
- Exalt His majesty (Psalm 95:3).
- Praise His creation and power (Psalm 95:4-5).
- Acknowledge Him in all things and submit to Him as your Lord and Creator (Psalm 95:6).
- Thank Him for being your Shepherd, submit to His care and listen to His voice (Psalm 95:7).

- Do not argue with the Lord or test Him, allowing your heart to become hardened (Psalm 95:8).
- Do not try the Lord's patience, instead praise Him for what you have already seen Him do, and do not argue with His plans (Psalm 95:9).
- Draw near to the Lord and listen and obey His instruction for you, trusting His plans and promises; trusting He is faithful (Psalm 95:10).

Today as your pray, continue to ask the Holy Spirit to give you wisdom and understanding as you spend time studying the Word. Enter into His rest. Seek it. Trust His promise of rest. Ask the Lord to expose your unbelief.

Father, we ask you to forgive any unbelief we may be carrying. We desire to pursue a deeper, fuller, more intimate relationship with Jesus Christ, our Savior. True rest comes from Him and we desire a life centered on Him and all that He is. Allow us to enter into His rest as we draw nearer to Christ.
In Jesus' Name,
Amen.

Week Five

Hebrews: Chapter 4:1-11

Chapter 3 concluded the recipe for entering into God's rest. It was unbelief that kept the Israelites from entering into the Promised Land and the rest God had available for them there (Hebrews 3:19). We must warn one another, out of love, to not allow distrust to slip into our lives and destroy the gifts God has prepared for us.

As we enter into this 4th Chapter of Hebrews, do not allow the difficulties of the present moment to overshadow the reality of God's promises. When we trust our own efforts and lean on our own understanding (Proverbs 3:5-6), instead of relying on Christ's power, we are in danger of missing the promised land rest.

Read Hebrews 4:1-11.

The following notes/questions will come from this chapter, unless, another passage of scripture is noted. Continue to journal and process all the Lord is teaching you as you center your life on Him.

Verse 1

In what way (or with what emotion) does verse 1 tell us to respond to the truth, that disbelief will make us fail to experience God's rest? We should fear experiencing unbelief. We should fear not trusting the Lord.

Read Luke 12:5, Philippians 2:12, and Romans 11:20.

We often think of fear as a negative thing. Anxiety and fear are different.

How do these passages about fear teach us a proper response to God?

Fear in the promises of God, make us fearless to the worries of this life.

As a little girl, I had a very cautious, overprotective, next door neighbor. She took a can of spray paint and painted a line across the cul-de-sac where her daughter and I rode our bikes, convincing us that crossing the line would mean certain death brought on by a teenage girl driving a sports car. Everything within my yard and theirs was within our limits of freedom, but we were taught to fear the road. We were taught to fear crossing the painted line. *Fear kept us from where we should not be.* In the same way, fearing unbelief keeps us within the bounds where we should not have to experience fear at all. Abiding in Him, centering our lives on Him, trusting and believing Him, is where freedom lives.

Verse 2

"Share the faith" or "joined in faith." When we profess faith in Jesus, we are united with Christ as well as to other believers.

Read 1Corinthians 12:12-13, Ephesians 2:11-22, Ephesians 4:3, and Philippians 2:1-2.

Verse 2-3

Read Exodus 34:6-7 and Numbers 14:8-9.

What was the Good News in these passages? The Israelites did not yet have the full story. They did not yet know Jesus or His death and resurrection like the Hebrew audience (or us), but they did have other promises that continue to remain true simply because the Lord never changes.

- God is merciful.
- God forgives sins.
- God promises rest.

- God promises joy for us who put our trust in Him.

What good are promises if we refuse to believe them? How would unbelief affect your living, in the midst of, waiting for promises fulfilled?

Journal about a time when you have experienced disbelief in God. What is the Lord saying to you now about your disbelief?

John Piper said:

"The Christian life is a life of day by day, hour by hour trust in the promises of God to help us and guide us and take care of us and forgive us and bring us into a future of holiness and joy that will satisfy our hearts infinitely more than if we forsake him and put our trust in ourselves or in the promises of this world. And that day by day, hour by hour trust in God's promises is not automatic. It is the result of daily diligence and it is the result of proper fear."

Verse 3-6

Rest has been ready for us since creation. Reflecting on the Old Testament, we can see that rest is continuously offered to God's people and rest remains available for us today.

Read Hebrews 4:9 again, followed by Psalm 95:7.

If you are a follower of Jesus, have surrendered to Him as your Savior, and have placed your faith in God, then, the promise of Sabbath rest is available for you- **today**. Just as His promise of rest remains, the consequences of disbelief remain as well.

As women, wives, mothers, friends, and servants, rest is a commodity most of us deeply desire and long for.

We live in a culture that appeals to the concept of rest: luxury sheets with high thread counts, memory foam mattresses, sleep aids, sleep masks, sound machines, even, essential oils are mass produced to appeal to the rest we crave. Physical rest is necessary to our physical health.

How much more valuable do you believe spiritual rest is to your spiritual health and development?

Verse 7

"That time is today." Now. Do not wait. The time has come. This is an appeal with urgency. This urgency should challenge and convict us into not delaying obedience.

"Today" is *always,* today. For example, we read this passage, *today,* which happens to be a Saturday, as I write this. And if you read it tomorrow, the "time is today," will continuously apply to our lives.

Belief in God is not a once and done thing. Belief is something we should cling to, day after day after day.

Verse 8-11

God has prepared various, beautiful types of rest for us.

Salvation Rest: Rest from our works, in an effort to, earn God's favor.

Eternal Rest: Being in the presence of God for all eternity.

Sanctification/Sabbath Rest: A rest from striving in the power of our flesh, in an ineffective effort to attain godliness.

In your personal study time, please Read Romans 7 and 8. Reflect on the ways in which living to fulfill the law (striving and rule keeping), vary from the ways we are able to live in the Spirit. Journal your observations. Prepare to discuss your realizations within your small group.

When we are not deliberate and diligent to enter God's rest, then, we are following the path of the Israelites.

Read Hebrews 3:19 again.

What kept the Israelites from entering His rest? Unbelief will keep us from the rest available to us.

BELIEF = REST

Read the following passages and pay careful attention to the word "belief" or "believe" in each passage.
Mark 16:15-16
John 3:16, 36
John 14:1
John 20:29-31
Romans 10:9-10

What are some of the promises of belief found in these verses and how are they connected with the rest God has prepared?

I pray that this week each of us will fall on our knees before the holy Lord and that we will ask Him to expose and deal with our areas of unbelief.

Do you believe He can heal your loved one? Do you believe He will provide for your need? Do you believe He truly is who He says He is? Do you believe He can breathe new life into your marriage, deliver your child from bondage, restore your brokenness? Do you believe He has prepared rest for you and that His boundaries give you freedom? Do you believe that striving can stop, and faith *is actually enough*?

Take some time to confess areas of unbelief. Take some time to reflect on what the Lord is revealing to you. The Lord desires to take from you all that binds you and weighs you down.

I am praying this week our belief is grown and our hope is centered on all that Christ is.

Week Six

Hebrews: Chapter 4:12-16

The writer of Hebrews is challenging the audience to avoid turning our backs to the promises of God and forfeiting the rest of Jesus Christ. Even, in the midst of a spiritual wilderness and the valleys of this life, our present and momentary struggles should not overshadow the reality of God's promises.

2Corinthians 4:17-18 says, "For our light and momentary troubles are achieving for us an eternal glory that far outweighs them all. So, we don't look at the troubles we can see now; rather, we fix our gaze on things that cannot be seen. For the things we see now will soon be gone, but the things we cannot see will last forever." Eternal glory; eternal rest. We must be diligent to hear the Word of God, study the Word of God, believe and trust the Word of God, and allow it to satisfy us in our waiting and in our longing.

Read Hebrews 4:12-16.

The following notes/questions will come from this chapter, unless, another passage of scripture is noted. Pause to pray before you begin to read this passage. Ask the Lord to allow you to understand what it is He has for you to learn. Take time to pause and center your focus on Him. Journal any realizations you have, questions that may arise, and any thoughts you have as you study.

Verse 12

"Alive & active." "Alive & powerful." "Living & active." "Quick & powerful."

Each translation uses the combination of two adjectives to describe the Word of God. If anything is living, but not active, it is considered to be dormant; alive, but not actively growing, as if asleep.

How many of us claim to believe His Word and desire His rest, *yet,* live spiritually dormant? His Word is alive and active, **but is our faith**?

Read Jeremiah 23:29, Isaiah 55:11, 1Thessalonians 2:13, and John 12:48.

What is being said about "His Word" in each of these passages? How are these passages connected to Hebrews 4:12?

God's Word truly is Good News. His promises and the warnings of His judgement are sharp, living, and active enough to penetrate our hearts and expose our sinfulness, in light of, His holiness. Nothing else in all of creation has this power. The Word of God is the only thing strong enough to break the bondage of sin and deception.

The Word of God is our only hope.

Anyone who is diagnosed with cancer receives a PET Scan. PET Scanners work by revealing how the body is functioning and uncovering areas with abnormal metabolic activity. The hidden cancer cells draw in, absorb, and metabolize the glucose solution exposing their prior unseen presence. The Word of God is like glucose pulsing through your veins.

His Word searches out, examines, and exposes every cell within you masquerading as "healthy". All the while, these cells are secretly destroying you from the inside out. His Word exposes who we are *and* who we are not. It penetrates our core both morally and spiritually. His Word distinguishes what lies hidden within us, both our sinfulness, as well as, our righteousness.

Journal your thoughts.

What has God's Word revealed or exposed within you? How does this make you feel?

Verse 13

Read 1Samuel 16:7, Ecclesiastes 12:14, Jeremiah 2:22, and Luke 8:17.

How does it make you feel to not just know God, but to be *fully* known by God?

Verse 14

The greatness and wholeness of Jesus is expressed in this verse by Him being named as both "Son of God" and "High Priest." Previously, in Hebrews Chapter 2, we studied how Jesus's death tore the veil that separated people from the presence of God. Jesus made our final atonement and gave us complete and unending access to the Lord as our ultimate and final High Priest.

Read 2Corinthians 5:21.

What thoughts or emotions come to mind as you reflect on Jesus exchanging His righteousness for your sin?

Verse 14 & 16

In these two verses, we are given two commands by the writer. Read these verses again and look for the commands.

Hold firmly and **come boldly**.

These sound like the fruit of belief to me. We are being warned again and again to not drift away, to tremble with fear at our disbelief, to not allow disobedience to separate us from the promises of

God. Faith is what allows us to hold firmly and to approach Him boldly.

Verse 15

Jesus was fully human and took on flesh to live in this sinful world. He encountered outside temptations of various kinds, yet, internally, He did not possess the same sin nature that you and I carry with us each day. Charles Spurgeon said this regarding Hebrews 4:15:

"Do not imagine that if the Lord Jesus had sinned, he would have been any more tender toward you; for sin is always of a hardening nature. If the Christ of God could have sinned, He would have lost the perfection of His sympathetic nature. It needs perfectness of heart to lay self all aside, and to be touched with a feeling of the infirmities of others."

Verse 16

Since Jesus is God and our High Priest and He is compassionate and understanding towards our weaknesses, we are now offered this invitation to prayer. Prayer is how the Christian approaches the throne of God. He has invited us to come to Him, reverently, as our King and confidently as our Lord.

Thrones depict royalty, prestige, power, and authority, and in 70 A.D., the audience would have considered the throne to also be a place of judgement and justice. In this verse we are not being invited to the throne of judgement, rather, we are welcomed to the throne of our "gracious God." The Throne of Grace calls us to draw near. At this throne we are given *and* called to receive His mercy. Mercy is God withholding what we do deserve: *condemnation, death, hell, and eternal separation from Him.* Grace is God giving us what we do not deserve: *forgiveness, righteousness, redemption, salvation, and rest.* Mercy is deliverance from judgment. Grace is extending kindness to the unworthy.

At His throne, we will "find grace to help us when we need it most."

This week, I was talking with friends and we began a conversation about painful things like, people we know burying their children or wives or losing their husbands.

I confessed that singing, "It Is Well with My Soul," is always a song of conviction and confession for me. Could I sing those words if the Lord allowed me to lose my husband? Bury a child? Lose my home?

I want to believe that He would be enough and that my faith would not falter, but the thought of enduring that pain scares me and so, I confess it to the Lord, and I confessed it to my friends. One of my friends said, "Katie, you haven't been given the grace to deal with that type of loss because you have not needed it. If you needed that grace, He would supply it."

So much wisdom in her words.

I believe she is right. And I believe that is exactly what verse 16 is saying about grace when we need it the most.

This special grace is given as we need it, *but* it is only found as we boldly approach the throne of our gracious God.

My prayer for us is, as we study His living and active Word, we would be changed more and more into His image. I pray we will not only be made aware of the evil hiding within us, masquerading as goodness, but that He might also allow us to be made aware of the ways in which He is transforming us through His Word.

I am praying that we will begin to see our secret thoughts and desires reflecting the grace and mercy that He has given to us.

This week approach Him boldly and confidently. He has invited you to His Throne of Grace. Receive what He offers you. And when you need special grace, strength to endure, ask. He gives good gifts to His children.

I am praying too, that this study has either been fruitful as a faith foundation or a faith furtherance.

I am praying the time you have spent in study and in worship has either realigned you with the Lord or centered you on Him for the first time. We have been designed for an intimate relationship with God, forever. You and I were created for eternity and because of the perfect sacrifice of Jesus Christ, our sin was reconciled on the cross. This reconciliation gives us hope of forgiveness. Christ's death, burial, and resurrection seals us from hope to assurance.

IF you have never trusted Jesus Christ for the forgiveness of your sins, you can change that today. Tell the Lord of your need of Him. Confess your brokenness. Confess your belief that He is God and through Him, alone, comes forgiveness.

Your Savior can handle your junk. He welcomes it. He embraces it. He adores you. He chose you. He loves you.

I want to thank you for your commitment to this study and to one another.

I want to challenge you to press on in your faith. Gather with other believers. Study on your own. Journal. Pray. Worship.

All My Love

Notes

Week One/ Hebrews: Chapter 1

_____

_____

_____

_____

_____

_____

_____

_____

_____

_____

_____

_____

_____

_____

Notes

Week Two/ Hebrews: Chapter 2:1-4

_____

_____

_____

_____

_____

_____

_____

_____

_____

_____

_____

_____

Notes

Week Three/ Hebrews: Chapter 2:5-10

_____

_____

_____

_____

_____

_____

_____

_____

_____

_____

_____

_____

Notes

Week Four/ Hebrews: Chapter 3

_____

_____

_____

_____

_____

_____

_____

_____

_____

_____

_____

_____

_____

Notes

Week Five/ Hebrews Chapter 4:1-11

_____

_____

_____

_____

_____

_____

_____

_____

_____

_____

_____

_____

_____

Notes

Week Six/ Hebrews: Chapter 4:12-16

_____

_____

_____

_____

_____

_____

_____

_____

_____

_____

_____

_____